This book is dedicated to the lives lost at Pulse, and their families.

"If a bullet should enter my brain, let that bullet destroy every closet door."

— Harvey Milk

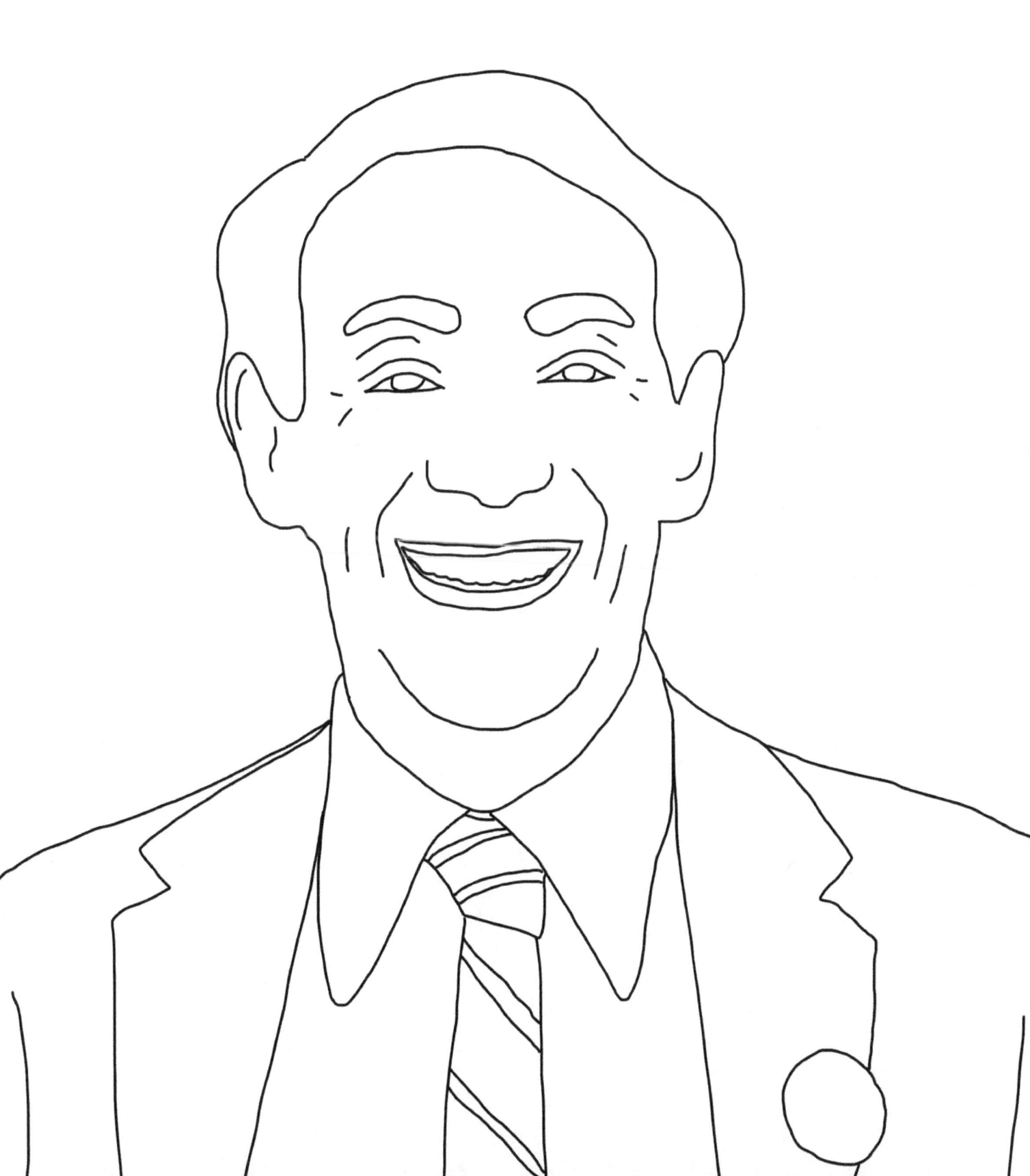

"When all Americans are treated as equal, no matter who they are or whom they love, we are all more free."

— Barack Obama

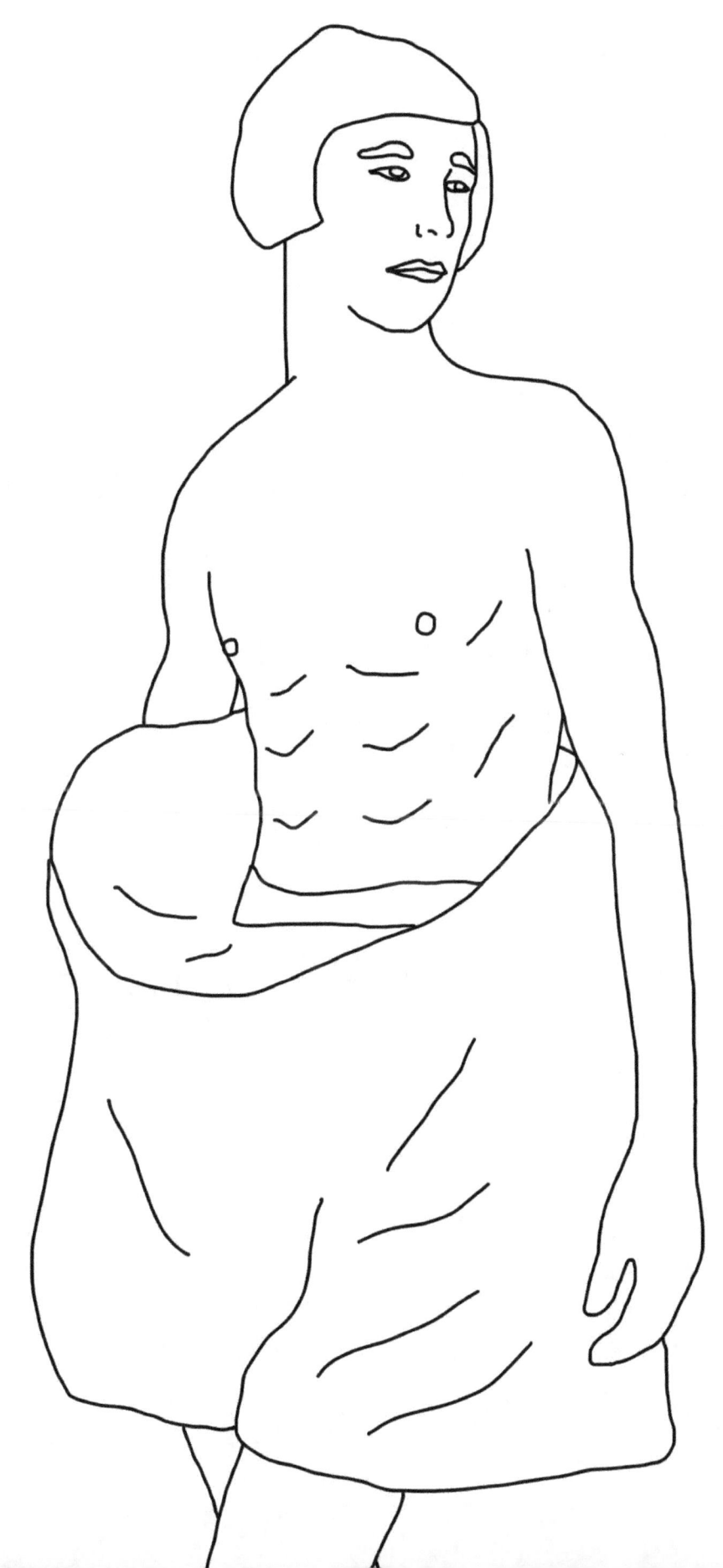

"In itself, homosexuality is as limiting as heterosexuality: The ideal should be to be capable of loving a woman or a man; either, a human being, without feeling fear, restraint or obligation."

— Simone de Beauvoir

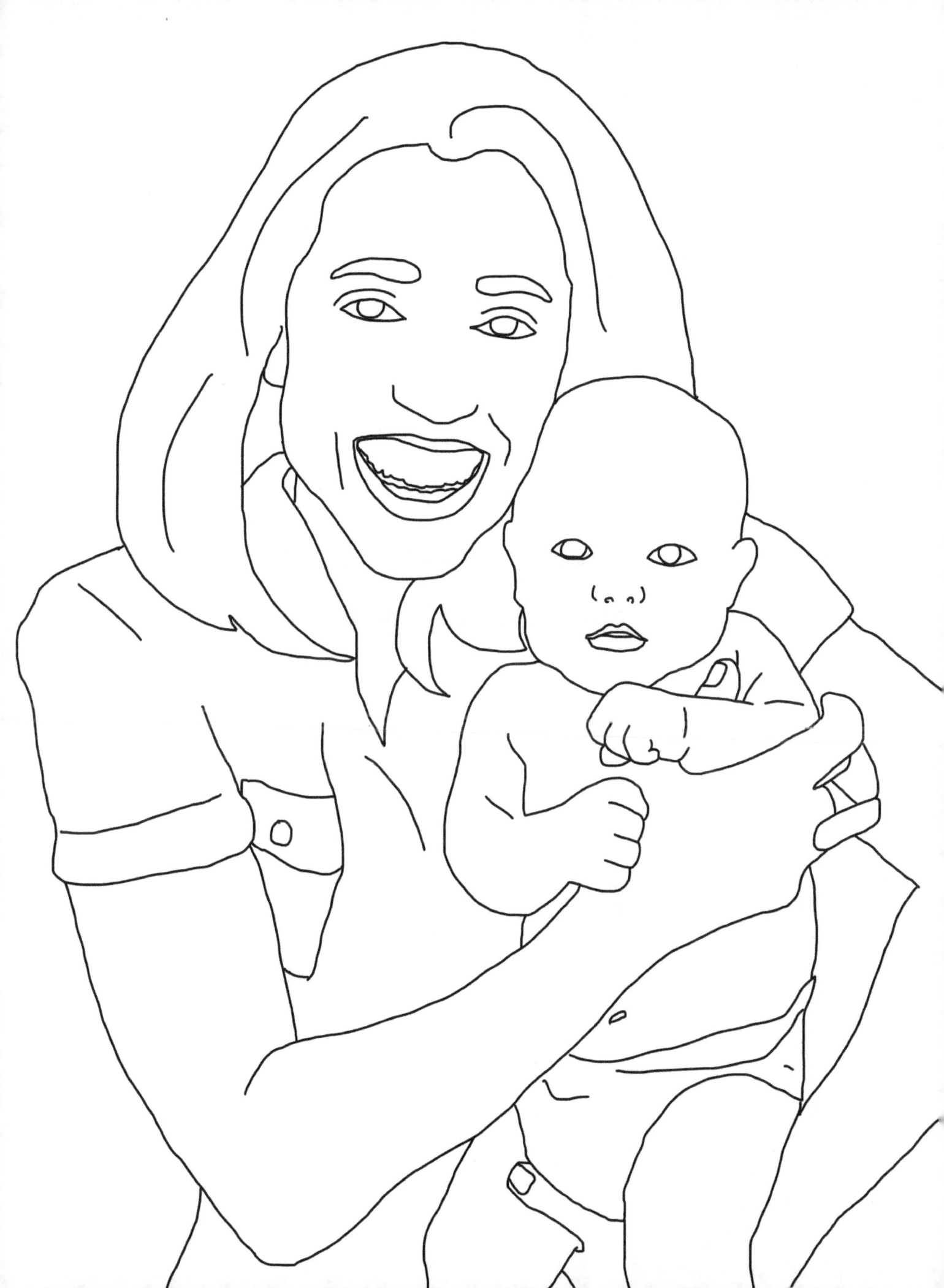

"What is straight? A line can be straight, or a street, but the human heart, oh, no, it's curved like a road through mountains."

— Tennessee Williams

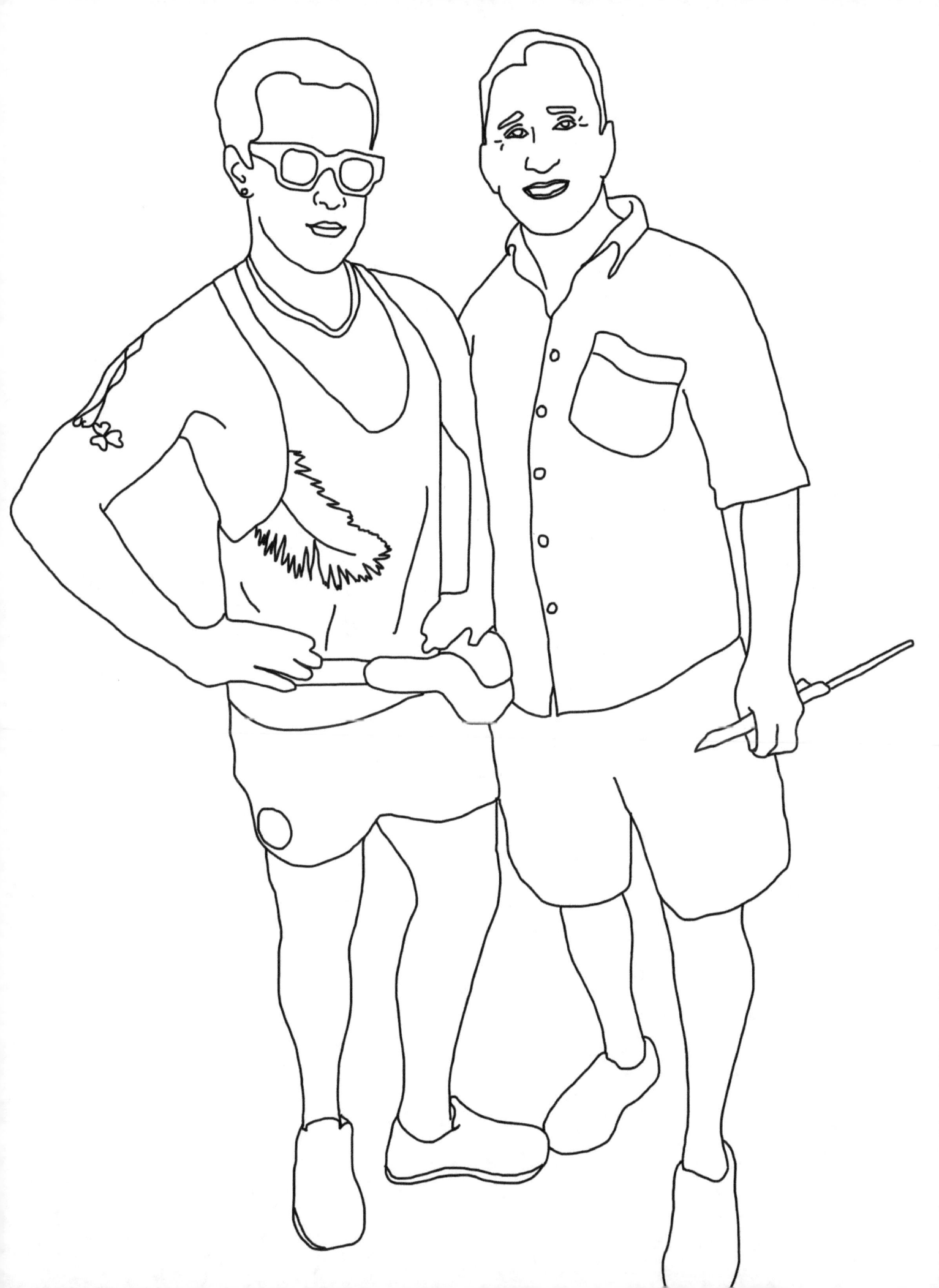

"Why is it that, as a culture, we are more comfortable seeing two men holding guns than holding hands?"

— Ernest Gaines

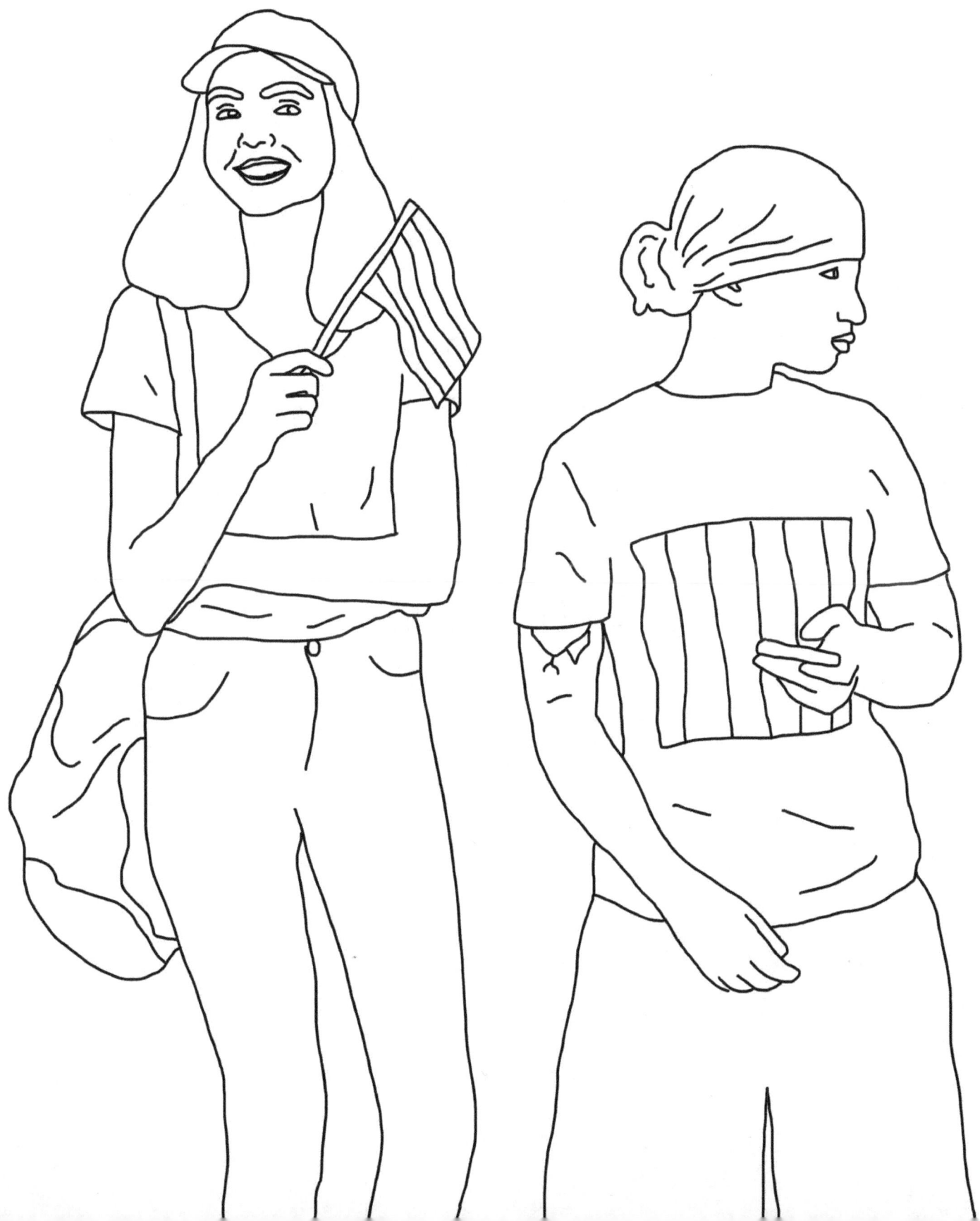

❝I've been embraced by a new community. That's what happens when you're finally honest about who you are; you find others like you.**❞**

— Chaz Bono

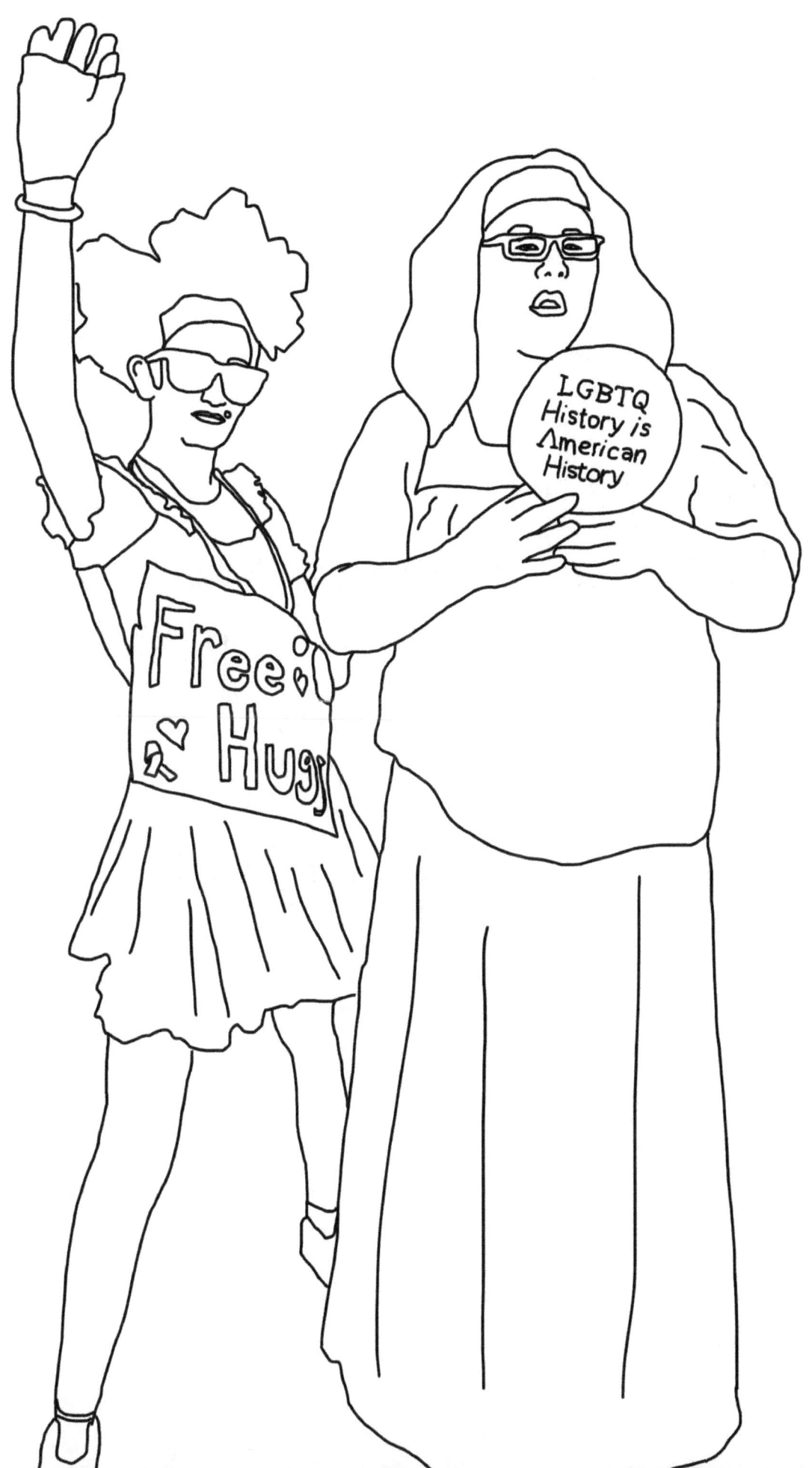

"We should indeed keep calm in the face of difference, and live our lives in a state of inclusion and wonder at the diversity of humanity."

— George Takei

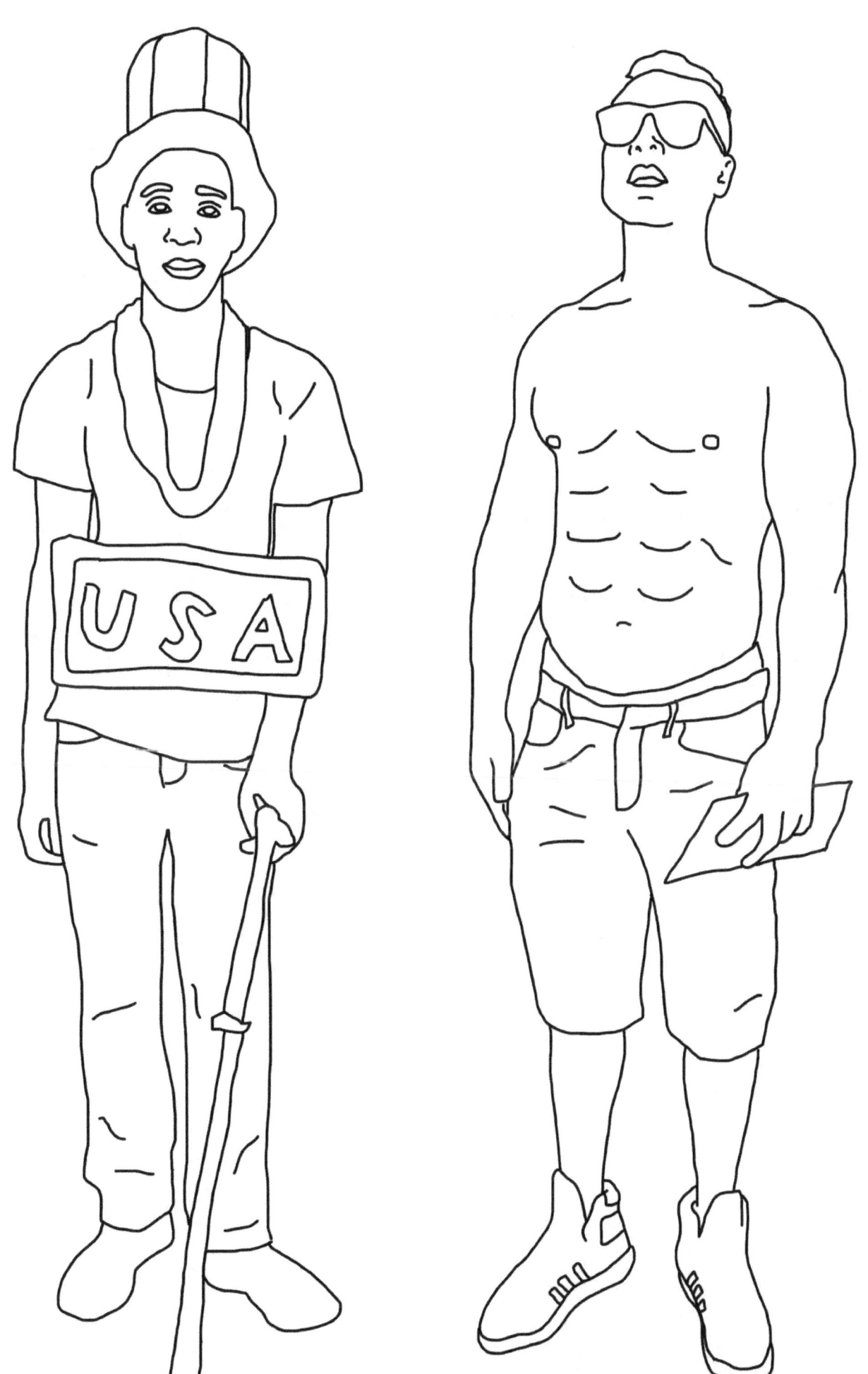

"Never be bullied into silence. Never allow yourself to be made a victim. Accept no one's definition of your life; define yourself.**"**

— Harvey Fierstein

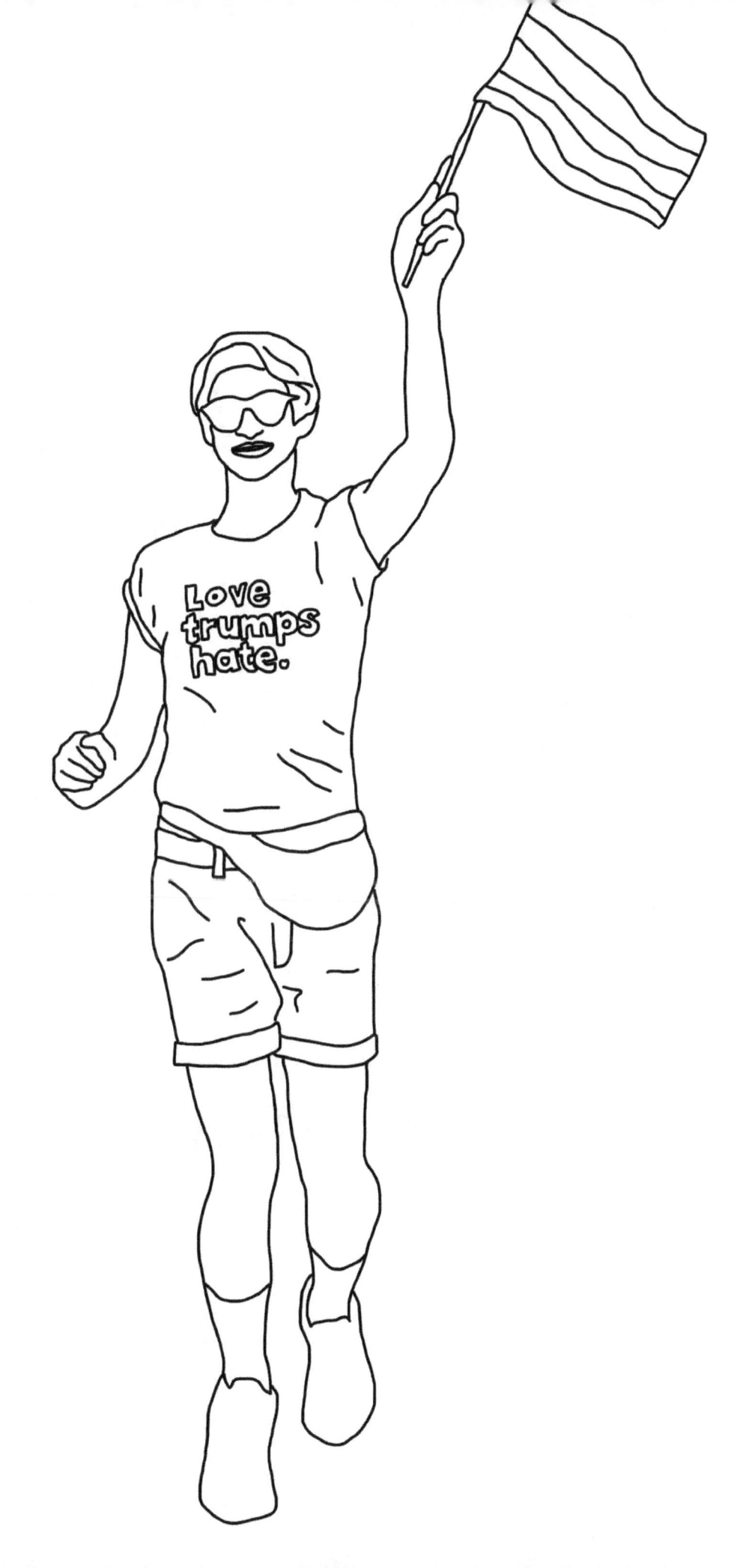

"All of us who are openly gay are living and writing the history of our movement. We are no more ~ and no less ~ heroic than the suffragists and abolitionists of the 19th century; and the labor organizers, Freedom Riders, Stonewall demonstrators, and environmentalists of the 20th century. We are ordinary people, living our lives, and trying as civil~rights activist Dorothy Cotton said, to 'fix what ain't right' in our society."

— Senator Tammy Baldwin

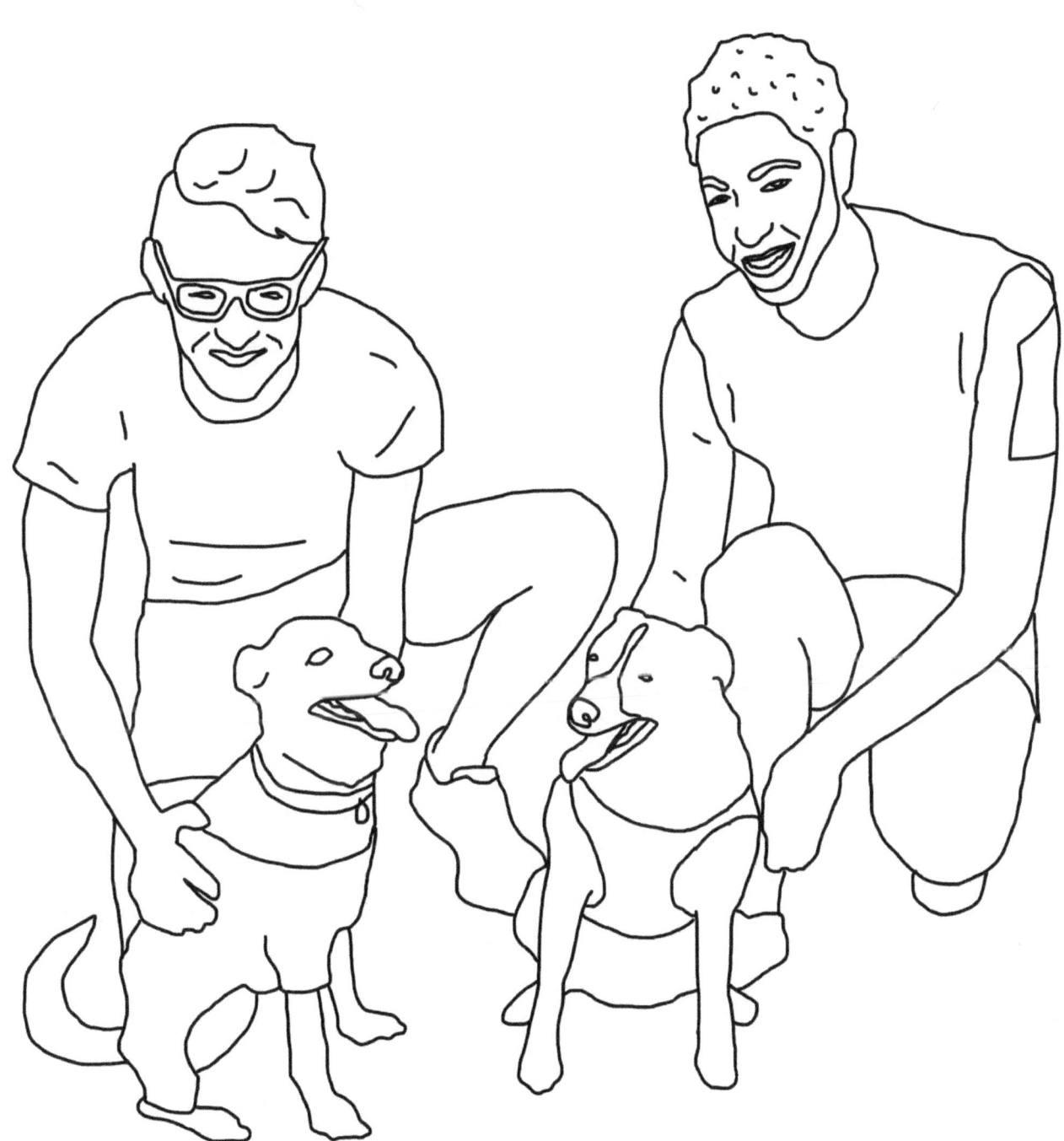

"I think being gay is a blessing, and it's something I am thankful for every single day.**"**

— Anderson Cooper

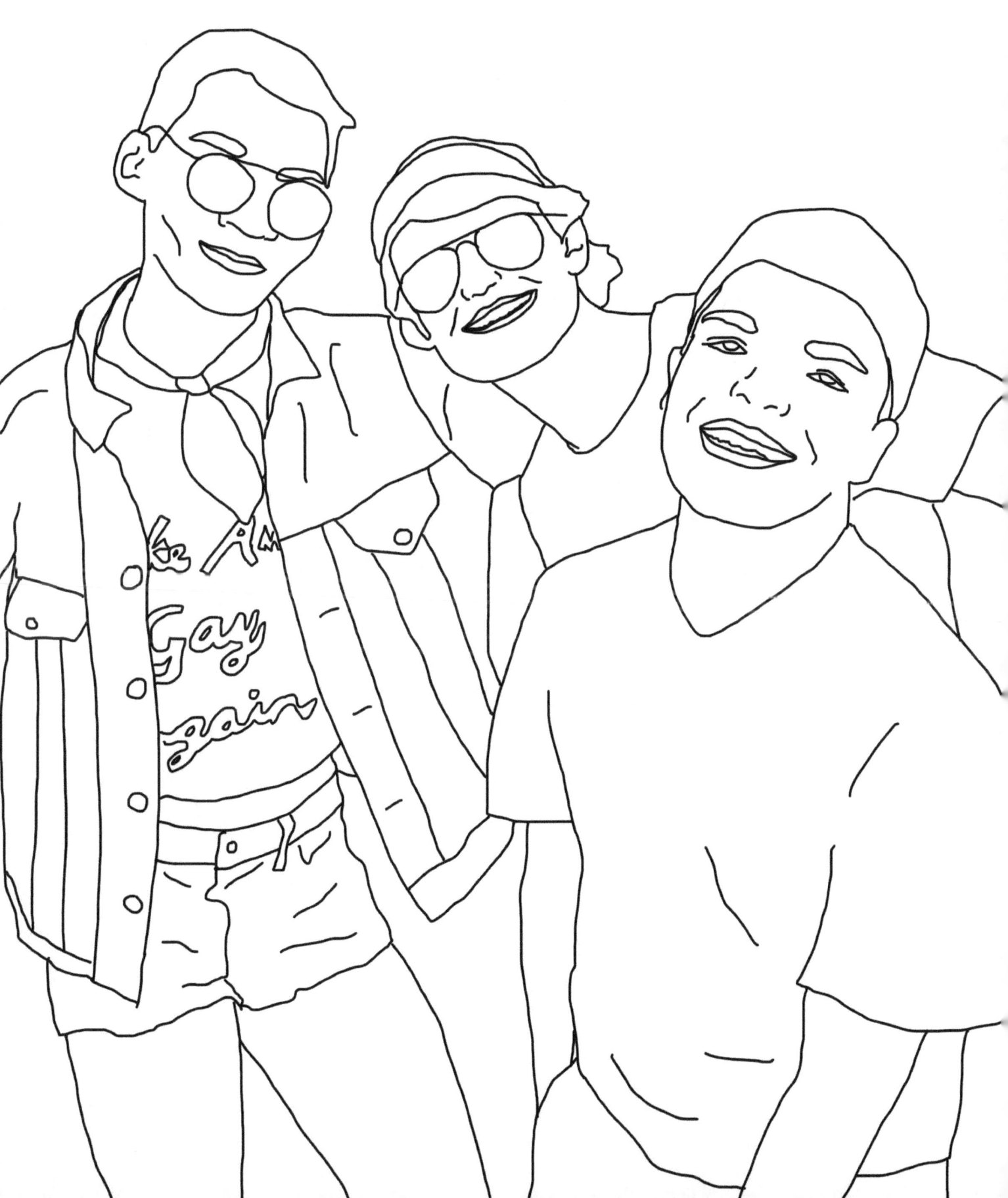

"Somebody, your father or mine, should have told us that not many people have ever died of love. But multitudes have perished, and are perishing every hour~and in the oddest places!~for the lack of it."

— Author James Baldwin

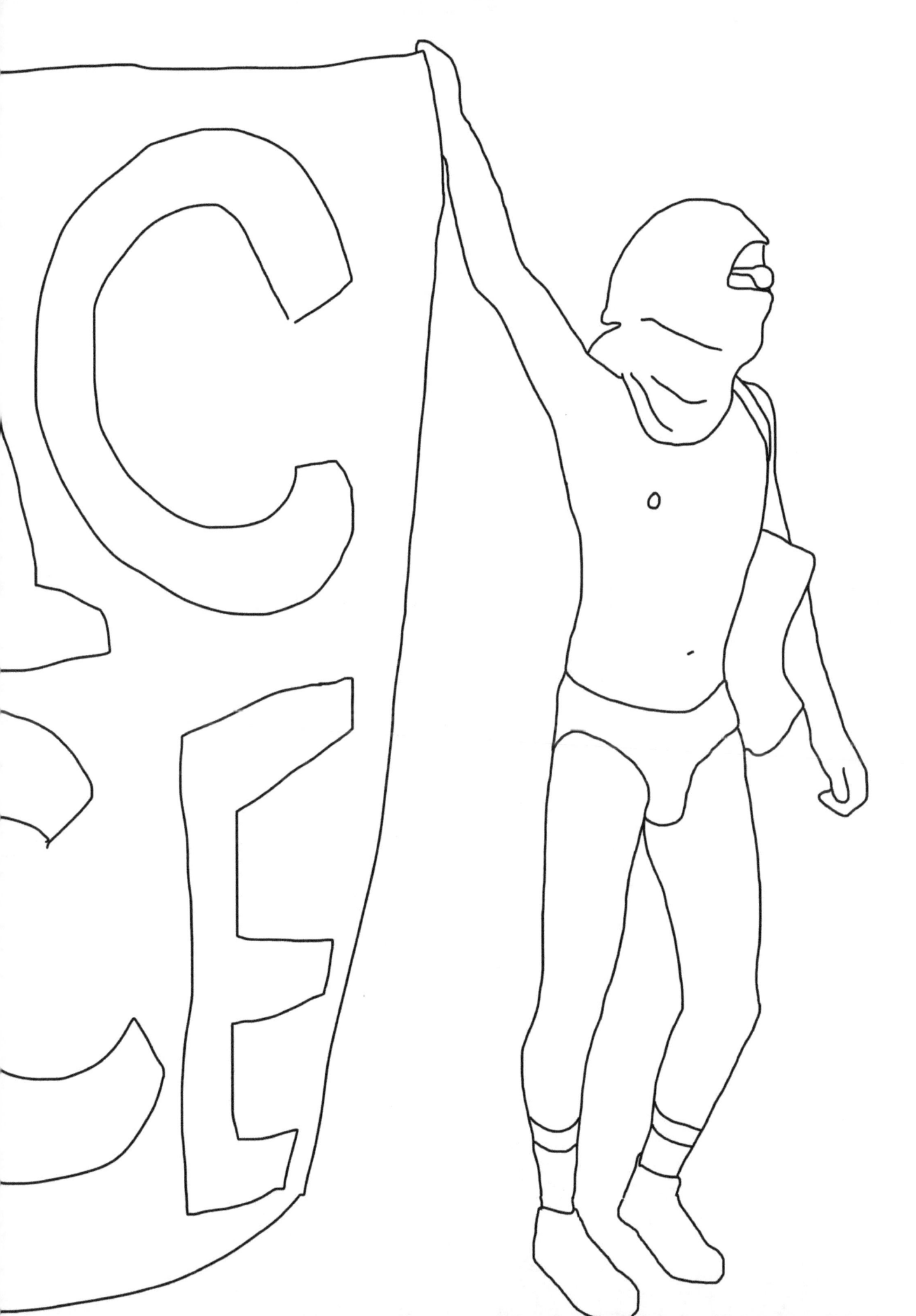

"We are shaped and fashioned by those we love."

— Goethe

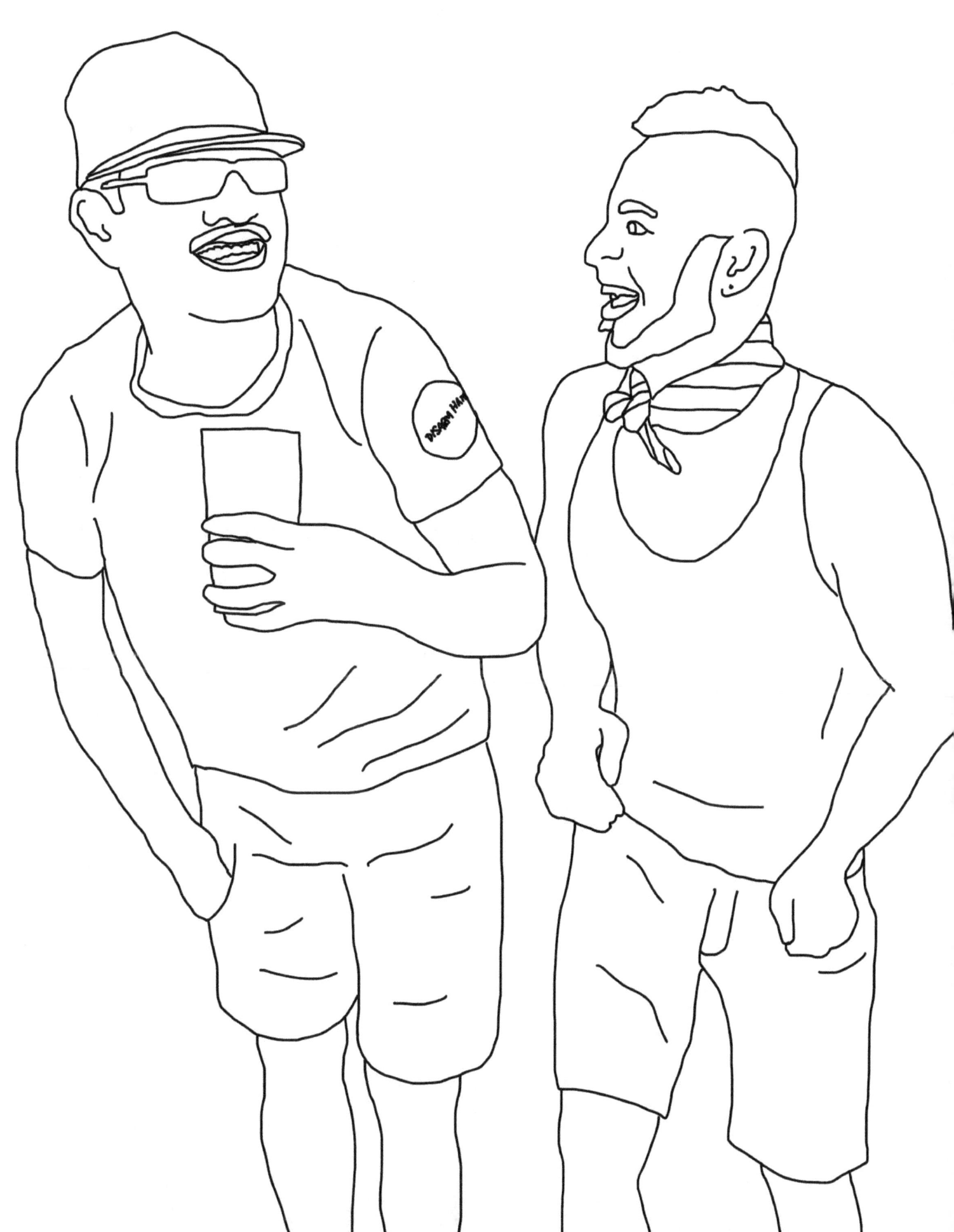

"At the touch of love everyone becomes a poet."

— Plato

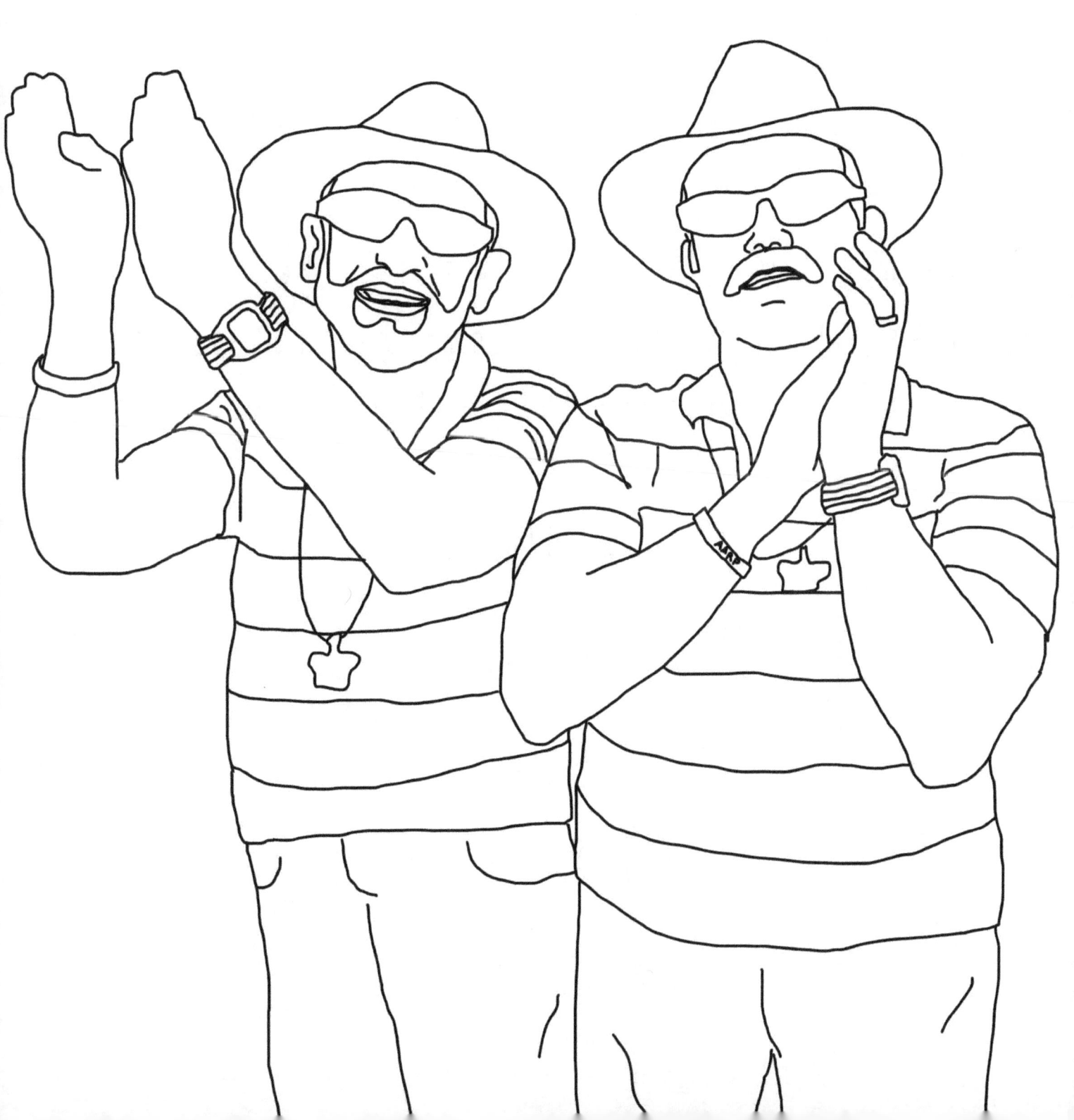

"The heart wants what it wants. There's no logic to these things. You meet someone and you fall in love and that's that."

— Woody Allen

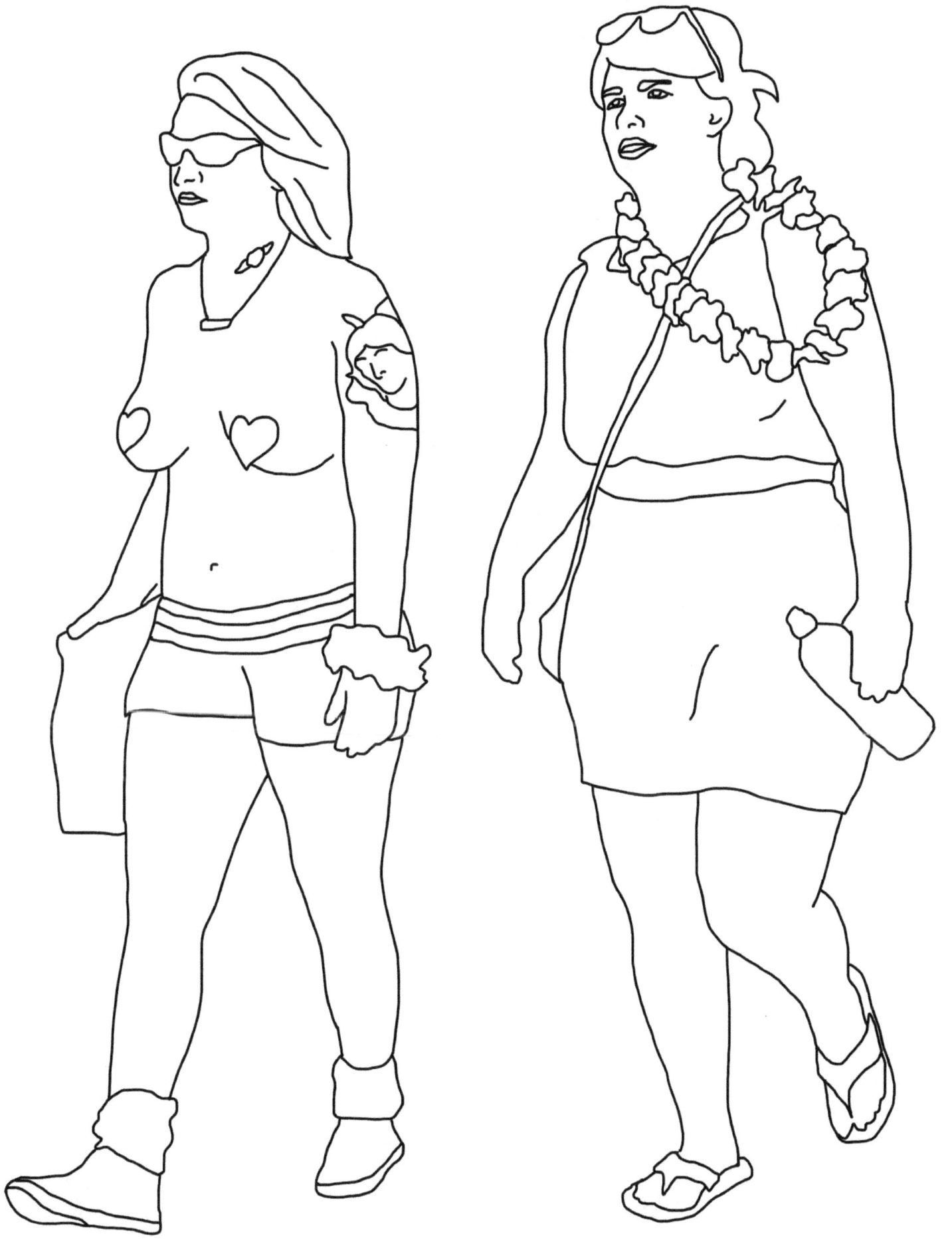

"All, everything that I understand, I only understand because I love.**"**

— Leo Tolstoy

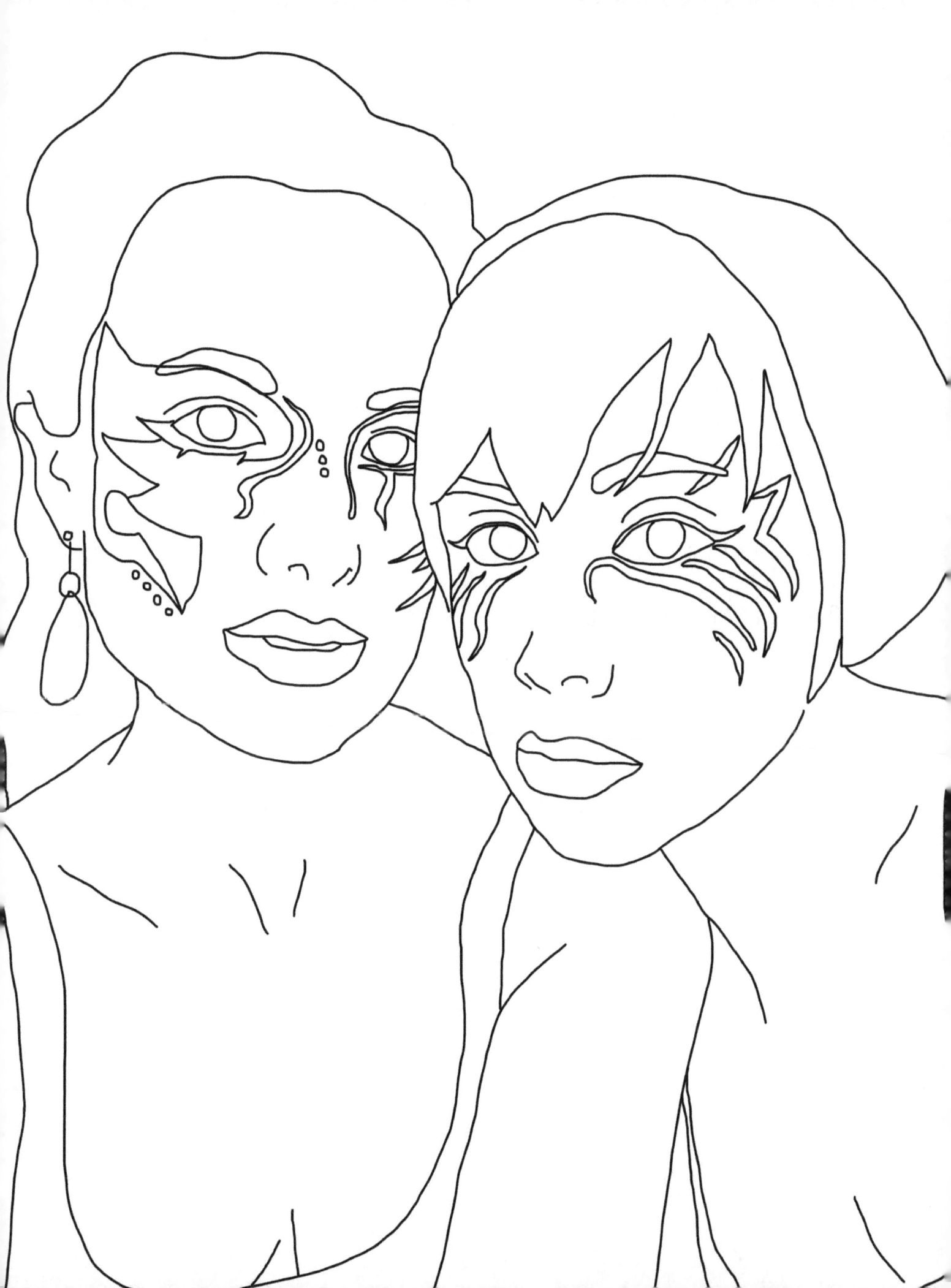

"The best and most beautiful things in this world cannot be seen or even heard, but must be felt with the heart."

— Helen Keller

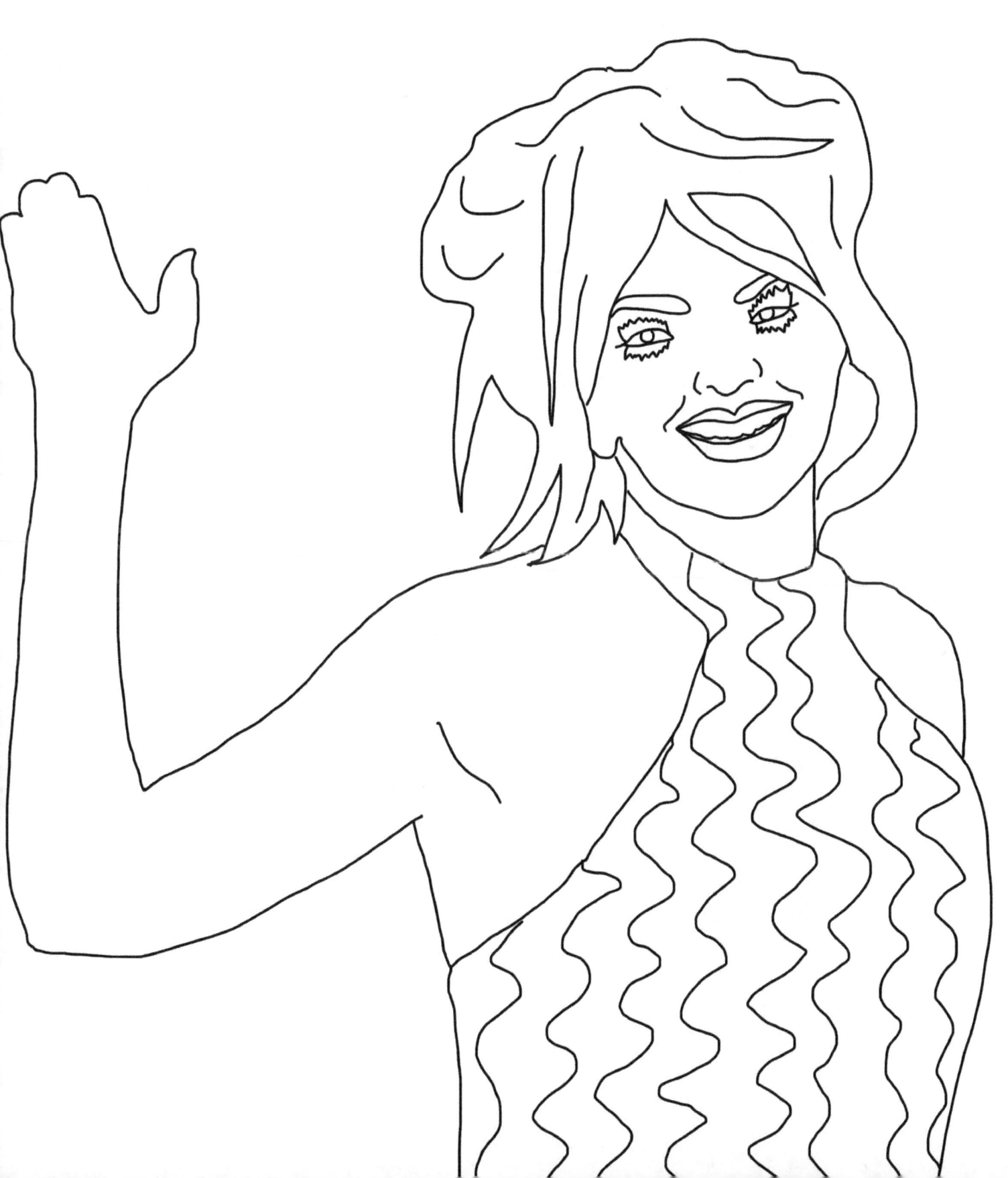

"There's no substitute for a great love who says, 'No matter what's wrong with you, you're welcome at this table.'"

— Tom Hanks

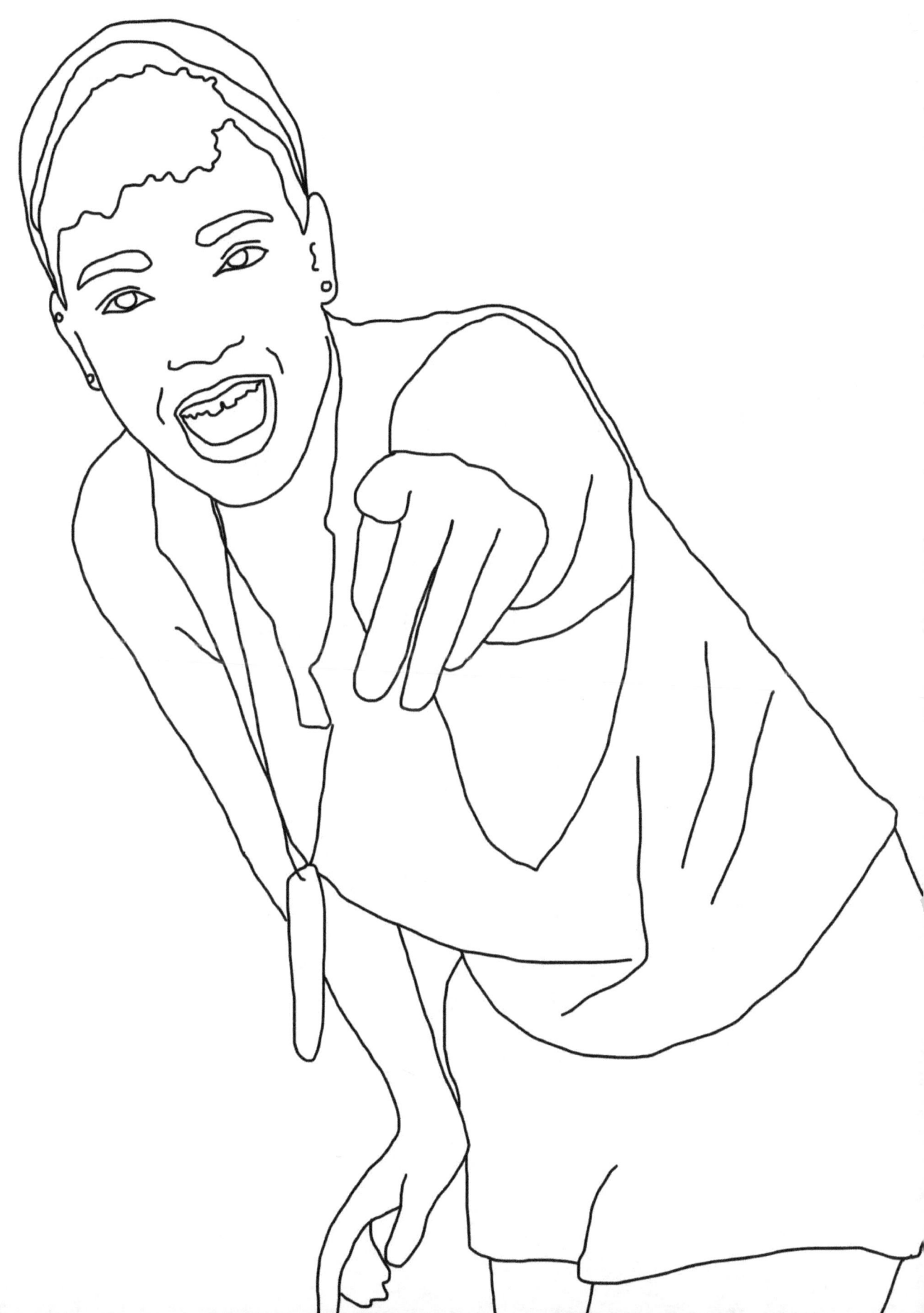

"Better to have lost and loved than never to have loved at all."

— Ernest Hemingway

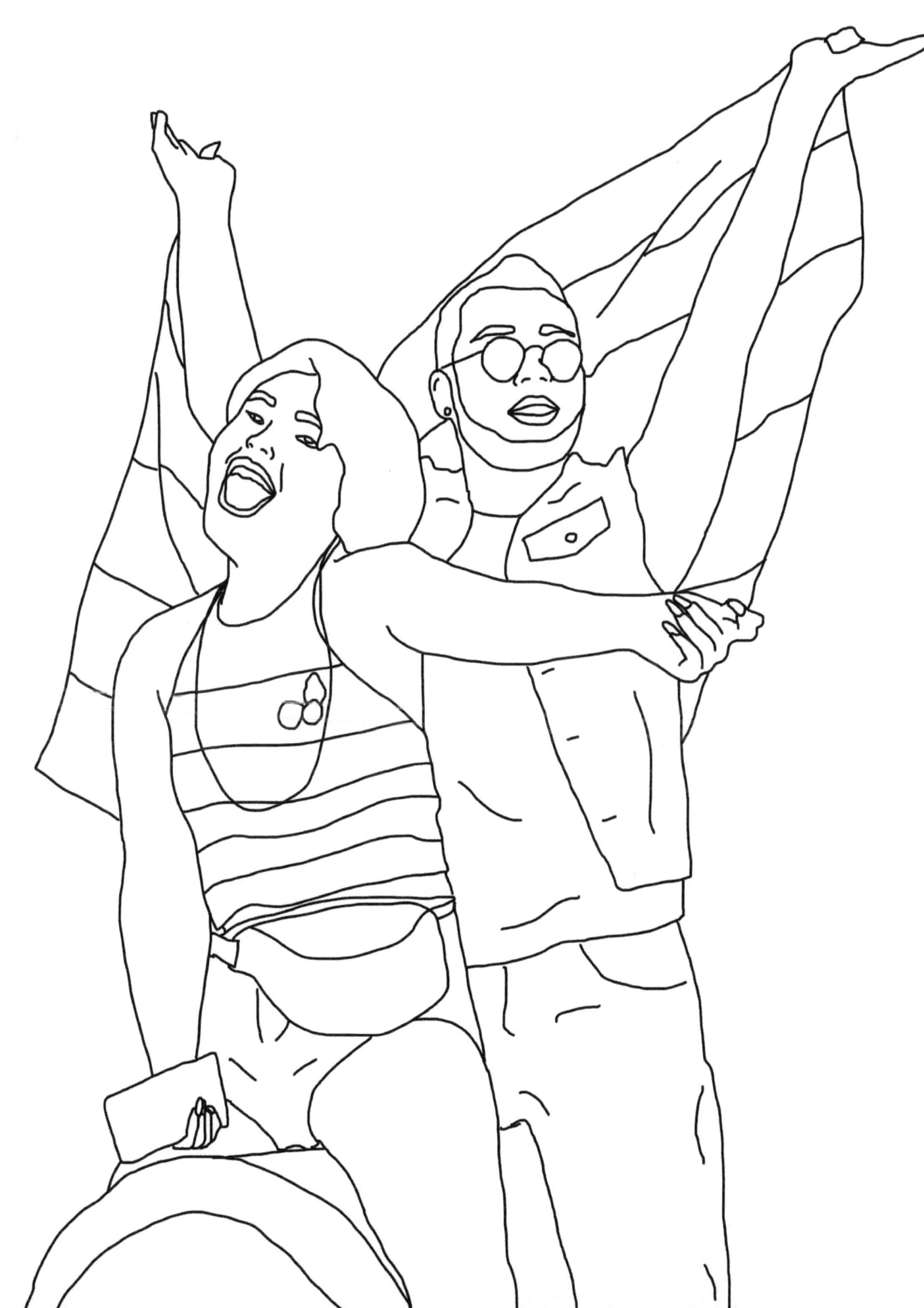

"You don't love someone for their looks, or their clothes, or for their fancy car, but because they sing a song only you can hear."

— Oscar Wilde

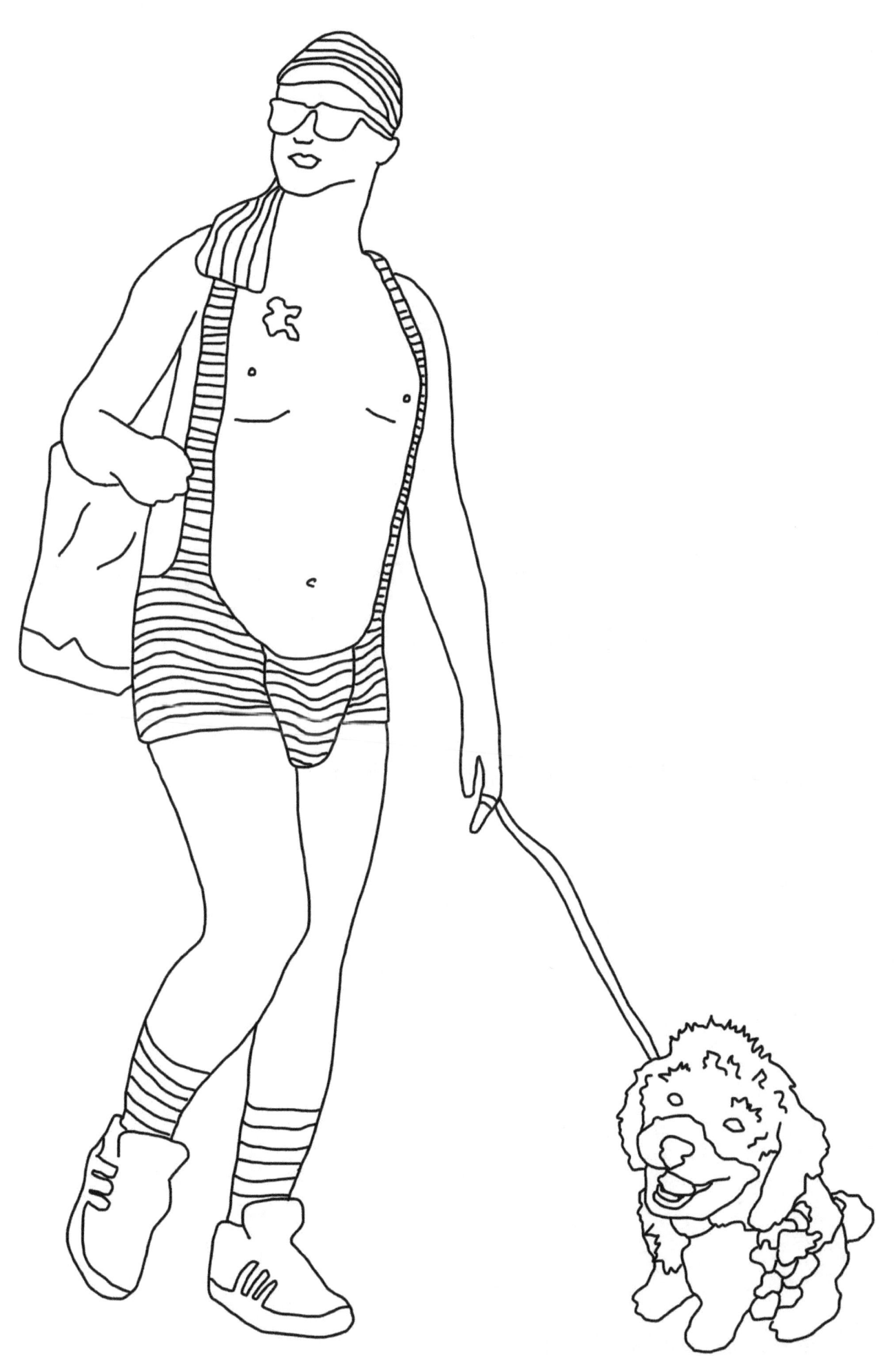

"I have decided to stick to love; hate is too great a burden to bear."

— Martin Luther King, Jr.

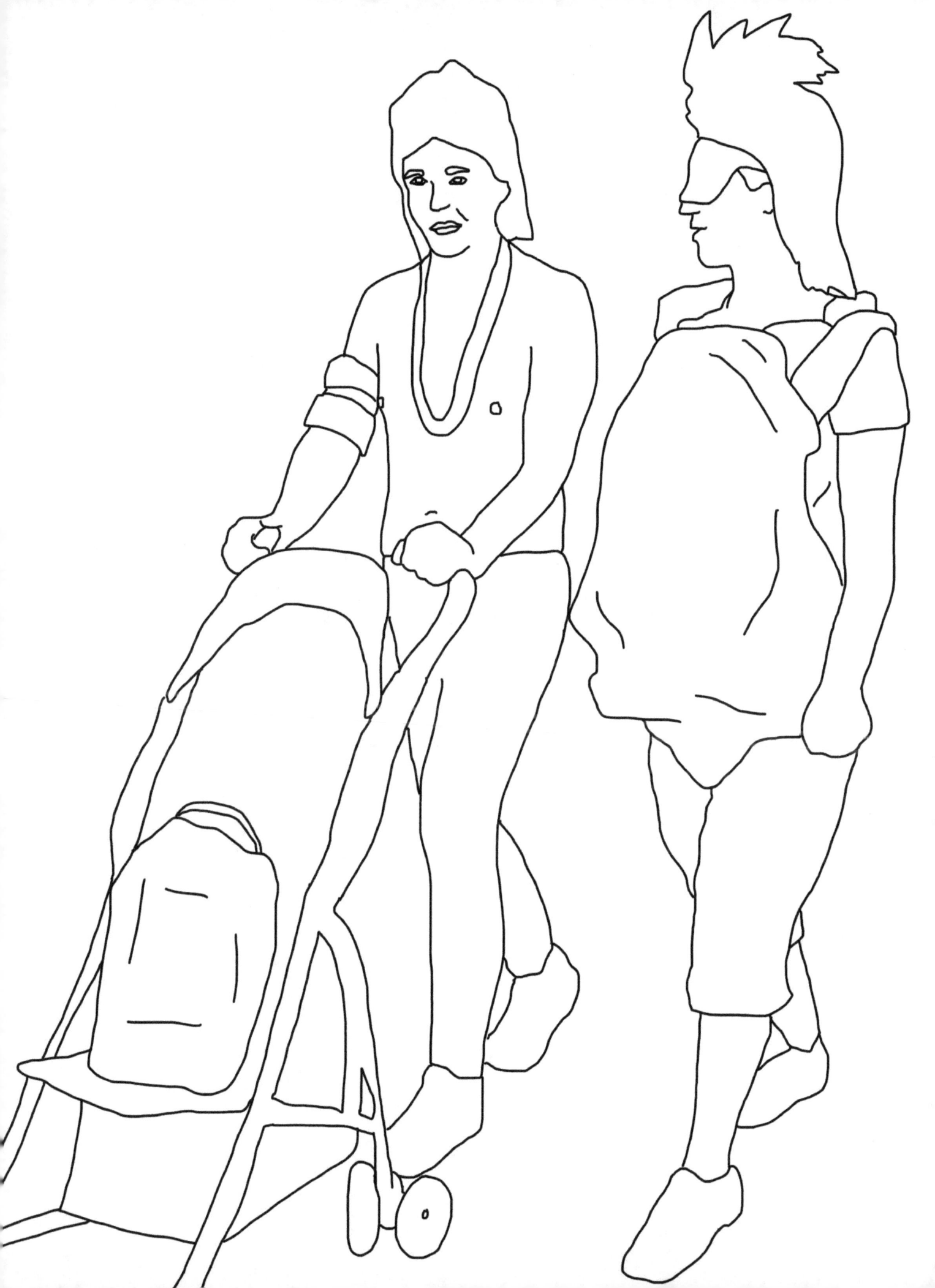

"One word frees us of all the weight and pain of life: That word is love."

— Sophocles

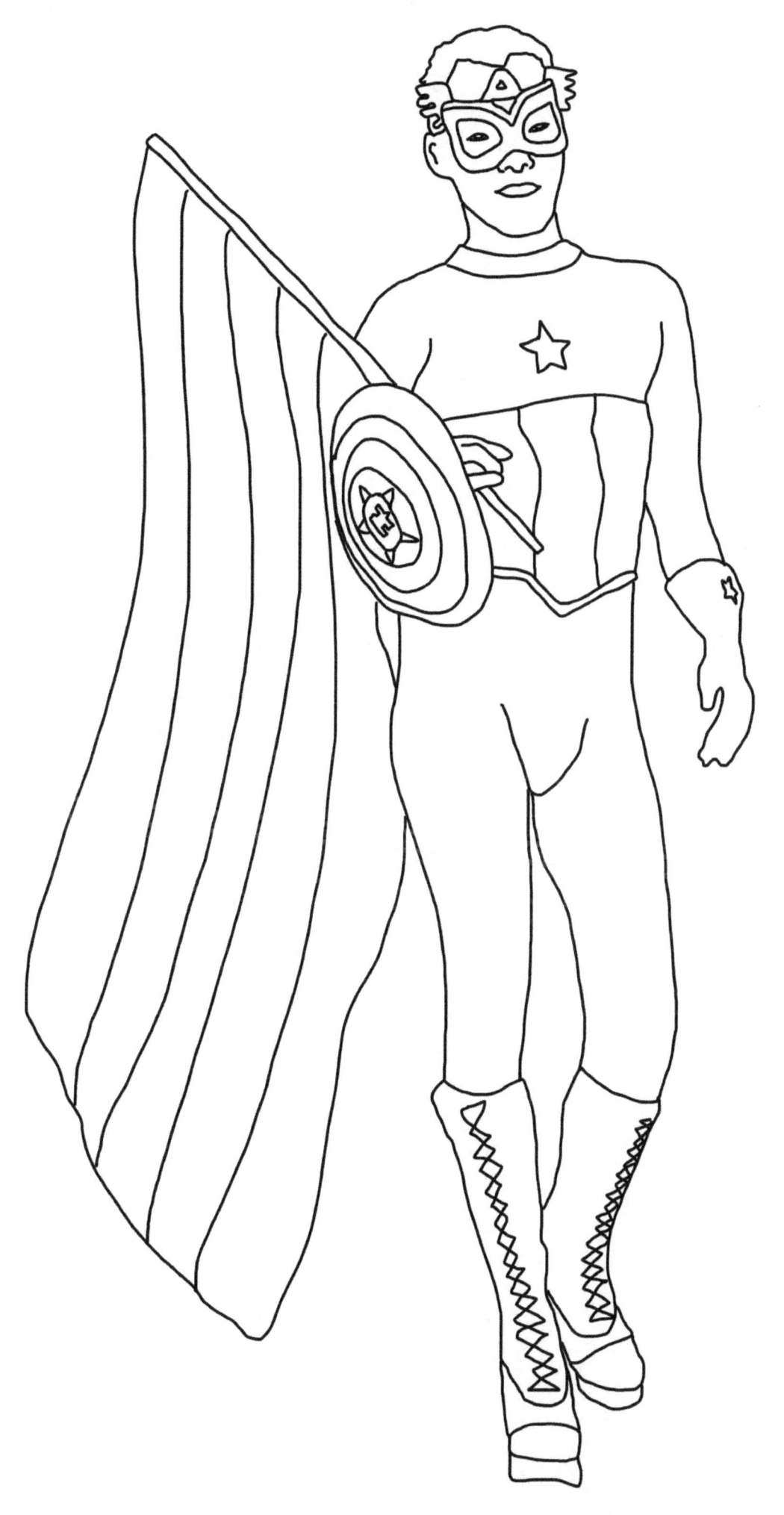

"If you don't love yourself, how in the hell you gonna love somebody else?"

— RuPaul

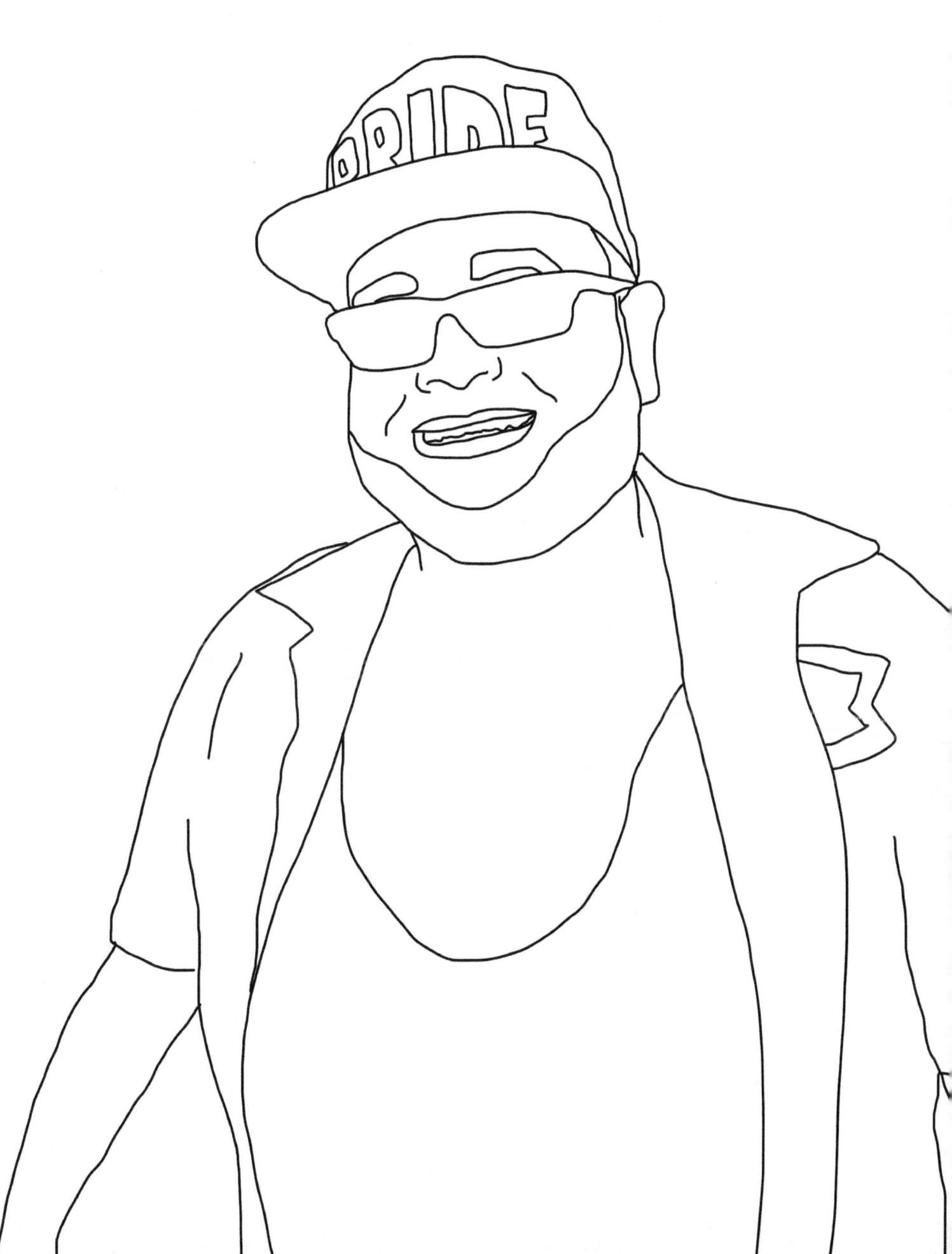

"Love is so short, forgetting is so long."

— Pablo Neruda

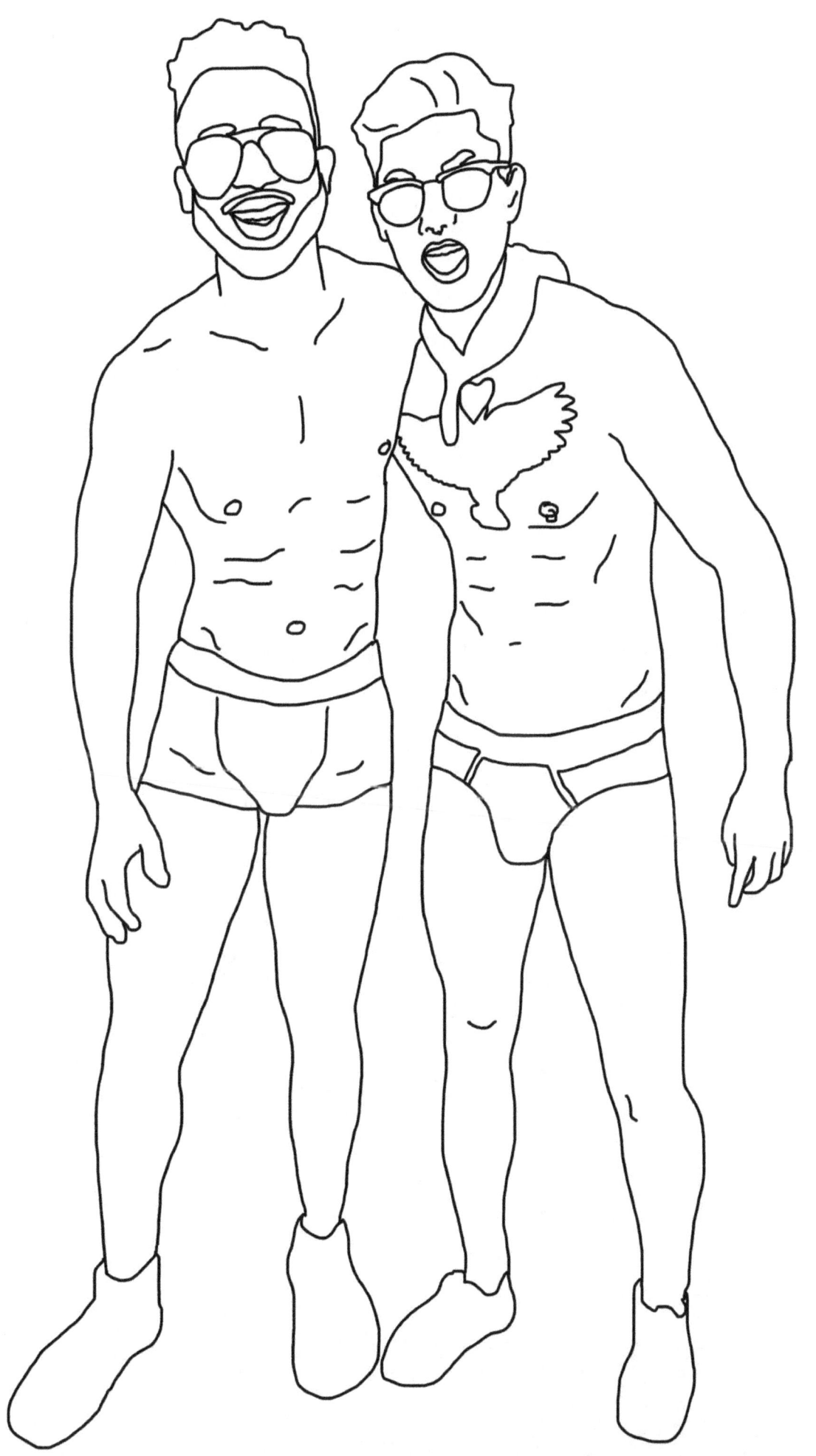

"Where there is love there is life."

— Mahatma Gandhi

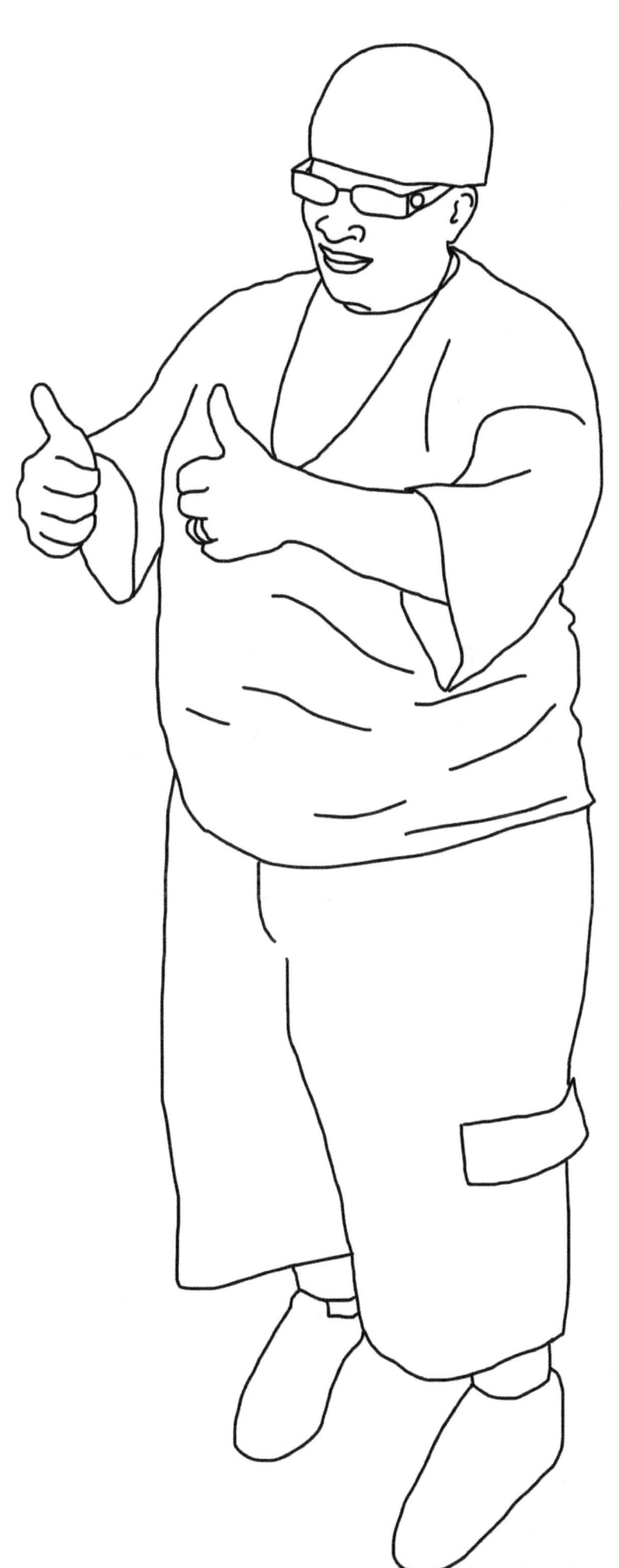

"The only queer people are those who don't love anybody."

— Rita Mae Brown

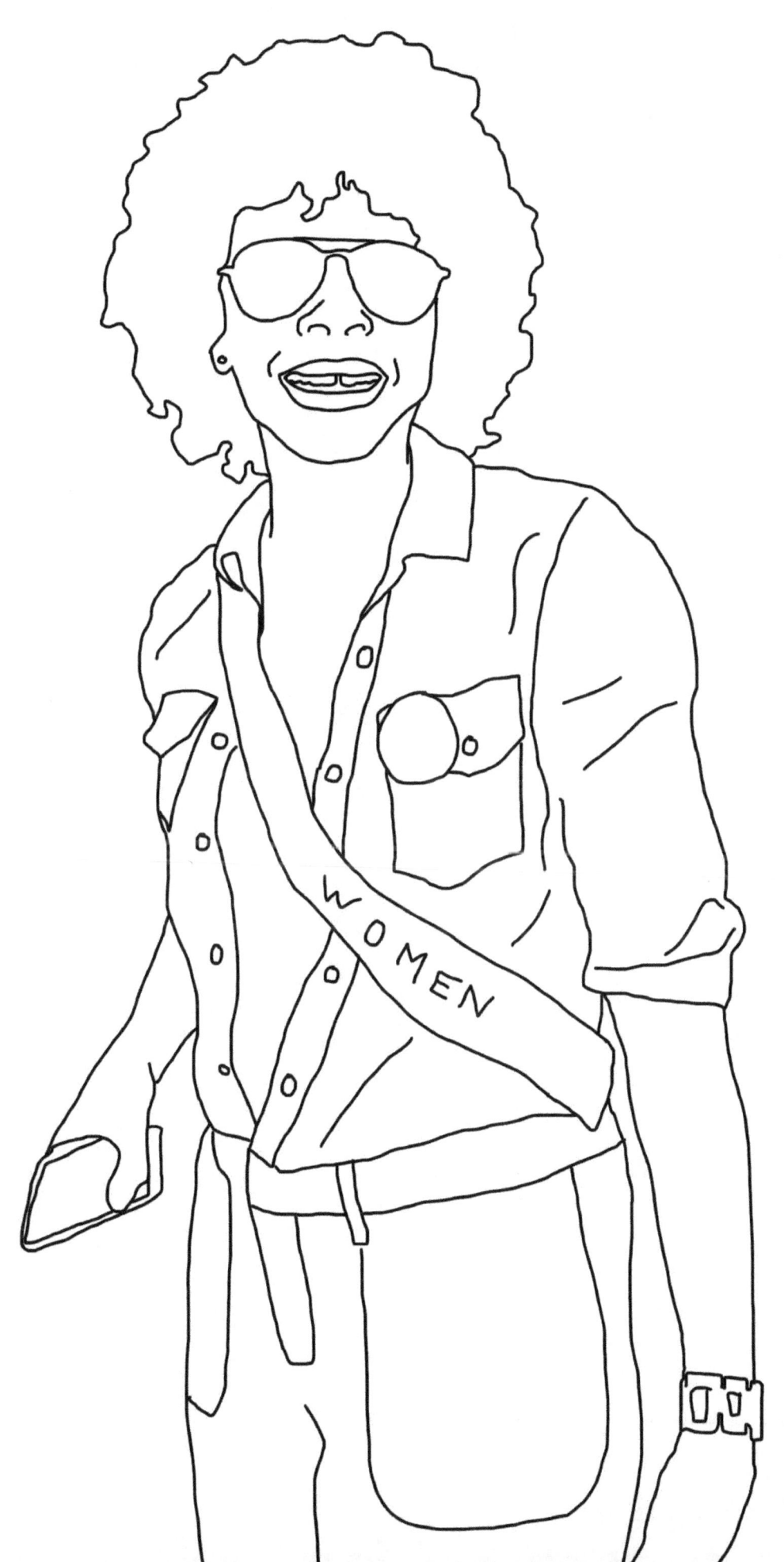

www.ingramcontent.com/pod-product-compliance
Lightning Source LLC
Chambersburg PA
CBHW080604190526
45169CB00007B/2869